TENOR SAX

101 POPULAR SONGS

Note: the keys in this book do not match the othe

Available for
FLUTE, CLARINET, ALTO SAX, TENOR SAX, TRUMPET,
HORN, TROMBONE, VIOLIN, VIOLA, CELLO

ISBN 978-1-4950-9026-4

HAL•LEONARD®
7777 W. BLUEMOUND RD. P.O. BOX 13819 MILWAUKEE, WI 53213

Visit Hal Leonard Online at
www.halleonard.com

CONTENTS

ABC

TENOR SAX

Words and Music by ALPHONSO MIZELL,
FREDERICK PERREN, DEKE RICHARDS
and BERRY GORDY

AFTERNOON DELIGHT

Tenor Sax

Words and Music by
BILL DANOFF

Moderately slow, in 2

AIN'T NO SUNSHINE

TENOR SAX

Words and Music by
BILL WITHERS

ALL YOU NEED IS LOVE

TENOR SAX

Words and Music by JOHN LENNON
and PAUL McCARTNEY

AIN'T TOO PROUD TO BEG

TENOR SAX

Words and Music by EDWARD HOLLAND JR.
and NORMAN WHITFIELD

ALL NIGHT LONG
(All Night)

TENOR SAX

Words and Music by
LIONEL RICHIE

Play 1st time only

ANOTHER BRICK IN THE WALL

TENOR SAX

Words and Music by
ROGER WATERS

Moderately

AT SEVENTEEN

TENOR SAX

Words and Music by
JANIS IAN

BAD, BAD LEROY BROWN

TENOR SAX

Words and Music by
JIM CROCE

BIG GIRLS DON'T CRY

TENOR SAX

Words and Music by BOB CREWE
and BOB GAUDIO

BILLIE JEAN

TENOR SAX

Words and Music by
MICHAEL JACKSON

BRIDGE OVER TROUBLED WATER

TENOR SAX

Words and Music by
PAUL SIMON

Moderately

CALIFORNIA DREAMIN'

TENOR SAX

Words and Music by JOHN PHILLIPS
and MICHELLE PHILLIPS

CARIBBEAN QUEEN
(No More Love on the Run)

TENOR SAX

Words and Music by KEITH VINCENT ALEXANDER
and BILLY OCEAN

CENTERFOLD

TENOR SAX

Words and Music by
SETH JUSTMAN

Bright Rock

COPACABANA
(At the Copa)

TENOR SAX

Music by BARRY MANILOW
Lyric by BRUCE SUSSMAN and JACK FELDMAN

CRACKLIN' ROSIE

TENOR SAX

Words and Music by
NEIL DIAMOND

DO YOU BELIEVE IN MAGIC

TENOR SAX

Words and Music by
JOHN SEBASTIAN

DOWNTOWN

TENOR SAX

Words and Music by
TONY HATCH

DOWN UNDER

TENOR SAX

Words and Music by COLIN HAY
and RON STRYKERT

DUST IN THE WIND

TENOR SAX

Words and Music by
KERRY LIVGREN

THE FIRST TIME EVER I SAW YOUR FACE

TENOR SAX

Words and Music by
EWAN MacCOLL

EASY

TENOR SAX

Words and Music by
LIONEL RICHIE

FREE BIRD

TENOR SAX

Words and Music by ALLEN COLLINS
and RONNIE VAN ZANT

Moderately

GENTLE ON MY MIND

TENOR SAX

Words and Music by
JOHN HARTFORD

Moderately bright, in 2

GIRLS JUST WANT TO HAVE FUN

TENOR SAX

Words and Music by
ROBERT HAZARD

GOD ONLY KNOWS

TENOR SAX

Words and Music by BRIAN WILSON
and TONY ASHER

GROOVIN'

TENOR SAX

Words and Music by FELIX CAVALIERE
and EDWARD BRIGATI, JR.

HAPPY TOGETHER

TENOR SAX

Words and Music by GARRY BONNER
and ALAN GORDON

HEY JUDE

TENOR SAX

Words and Music by JOHN LENNON
and PAUL McCARTNEY

I GET AROUND

TENOR SAX

Words and Music by BRIAN WILSON
and MIKE LOVE

I HEARD IT THROUGH THE GRAPEVINE

TENOR SAX

Words and Music by NORMAN J. WHITFIELD
and BARRETT STRONG

I SAW HER STANDING THERE

TENOR SAX

Words and Music by JOHN LENNON
and PAUL McCARTNEY

I STILL HAVEN'T FOUND WHAT I'M LOOKING FOR

TENOR SAX

Words and Music by
U2

I'M A BELIEVER

TENOR SAX

Words and Music by
NEIL DIAMOND

I WILL SURVIVE

TENOR SAX

Words and Music by DINO FEKARIS
and FREDERICK J. PERREN

IF

TENOR SAX

Words and Music by
DAVID GATES

IMAGINE

TENOR SAX

Words and Music by
JOHN LENNON

JESSIE'S GIRL

TENOR SAX

Words and Music by
RICK SPRINGFIELD

Moderately fast

JUST ONCE

TENOR SAX

Words by CYNTHIA WEIL
Music by BARRY MANN

53

KARMA CHAMELEON

TENOR SAX

Words and Music by GEORGE O'DOWD,
JONATHAN MOSS, MICHAEL CRAIG,
ROY HAY and PHIL PICKETT

KILLING ME SOFTLY WITH HIS SONG

TENOR SAX

Words by NORMAN GIMBEL
Music by CHARLES FOX

LADY

TENOR SAX

Words and Music by
LIONEL RICHIE

LAY DOWN SALLY

TENOR SAX

Words and Music by ERIC CLAPTON, MARCY LEVY and GEORGE TERRY

LEADER OF THE PACK

TENOR SAX

Words and Music by GEORGE MORTON,
JEFF BARRY and ELLIE GREENWICH

LEAN ON ME

TENOR SAX

Words and Music by
BILL WITHERS

Play cue 2nd time only.

LEAVING ON A JET PLANE

TENOR SAX

Words and Music by
JOHN DENVER

LET'S HANG ON

TENOR SAX

Words and Music by BOB CREWE,
DENNY RANDELL and SANDY LINZER

LET'S HEAR IT FOR THE BOY

from the Paramount Motion Picture FOOTLOOSE

TENOR SAX

Words by DEAN PITCHFORD
Music by TOM SNOW

LIKE A VIRGIN

TENOR SAX

Words and Music by BILLY STEINBERG
and TOM KELLY

THE LION SLEEPS TONIGHT

TENOR SAX

New Lyrics and Revised Music by GEORGE DAVID WEISS,
HUGO PERETTI and LUIGI CREATORE

LIVIN' ON A PRAYER

TENOR SAX

Words and Music by JON BON JOVI,
DESMOND CHILD and RICHIE SAMBORA

LOVE WILL KEEP US TOGETHER

TENOR SAX

Words and Music by NEIL SEDAKA
and HOWARD GREENFIELD

MANDY

TENOR SAX

Words and Music by SCOTT ENGLISH
and RICHARD KERR

MANEATER

TENOR SAX

Words and Music by SARA ALLEN,
DARYL HALL and JOHN OATES

MR. TAMBOURINE MAN

TENOR SAX

Words and Music by
BOB DYLAN

MONDAY, MONDAY

TENOR SAX

Words and Music by
JOHN PHILLIPS

MONY, MONY

TENOR SAX

Words and Music by BOBBY BLOOM,
TOMMY JAMES, RITCHIE CORDELL
and BO GENTRY

MY CHERIE AMOUR

TENOR SAX

Words and Music by STEVIE WONDER,
SYLVIA MOY and HENRY COSBY

MY GIRL

TENOR SAX

Words and Music by SMOKEY ROBINSON
and RONALD WHITE

NIGHTS IN WHITE SATIN

TENOR SAX

Words and Music by
JUSTIN HAYWARD

NIGHTSHIFT

TENOR SAX

Words and Music by WALTER ORANGE,
FRANNE GOLDE and DENNIS LAMBERT

ONE MORE NIGHT

TENOR SAX

Words and Music by
PHIL COLLINS

PHYSICAL

TENOR SAX

Words and Music by STEPHEN A. KIPNER
and TERRY SHADDICK

PIANO MAN

TENOR SAX

Words and Music by
BILLY JOEL

POUR SOME SUGAR ON ME

TENOR SAX

Words and Music by JOE ELLIOTT,
PHIL COLLEN, RICHARD SAVAGE,
RICHARD ALLEN, STEVE CLARK
and R.J. LANGE

REELING IN THE YEARS

TENOR SAX

Words and Music by WALTER BECKER
and DONALD FAGEN

RIGHT HERE WAITING

TENOR SAX

Words and Music by
RICHARD MARX

ROCKET MAN
(I Think It's Gonna Be a Long Long Time)

TENOR SAX

Words and Music by ELTON JOHN
and BERNIE TAUPIN

SAVING ALL MY LOVE FOR YOU

TENOR SAX

Words by GERRY GOFFIN
Music by MICHAEL MASSER

SHE DRIVES ME CRAZY

TENOR SAX

Words and Music by DAVID STEELE
and ROLAND GIFT

SHINY HAPPY PEOPLE

TENOR SAX

Words and Music by WILLIAM BERRY,
PETER BUCK, MICHAEL MILLS
and MICHAEL STIPE

SILLY LOVE SONGS

TENOR SAX

Words and Music by PAUL McCARTNEY
and LINDA McCARTNEY

SISTER CHRISTIAN

TENOR SAX

Words and Music by
KELLY KEAGY

Moderately slow

(Sittin' On)
THE DOCK OF THE BAY

TENOR SAX

Words and Music by STEVE CROPPER
and OTIS REDDING

SMOKE ON THE WATER

TENOR SAX

Words and Music by RITCHIE BLACKMORE,
IAN GILLAN, ROGER GLOVER,
JON LORD and IAN PAICE

SOMEBODY TO LOVE

TENOR SAX

Words and Music by
FREDDIE MERCURY

Moderately, in 2

SON-OF-A-PREACHER MAN

TENOR SAX

Words and Music by JOHN HURLEY
and RONNIE WILKINS

THE SOUND OF SILENCE

TENOR SAX

Words and Music by
PAUL SIMON

STAND BY ME

TENOR SAX

Words and Music by JERRY LEIBER,
MIKE STOLLER and BEN E. KING

Moderately, with a beat

SWEET DREAMS
(Are Made of This)

TENOR SAX

Words and Music by ANNIE LENNOX
and DAVID STEWART

SWEET HOME ALABAMA

TENOR SAX

Words and Music by RONNIE VAN ZANT,
ED KING and GARY ROSSINGTON

TAKE ME HOME, COUNTRY ROADS

TENOR SAX

Words and Music by JOHN DENVER,
BILL DANOFF and TAFFY NIVERT

THESE DREAMS

TENOR SAX

Words and Music by MARTIN GEORGE PAGE
and BERNIE TAUPIN

Moderately slow, in 2

THROUGH THE YEARS

TENOR SAX

Words and Music by STEVE DORFF
and MARTY PANZER

Slowly, in 2

TICKET TO RIDE

TENOR SAX

Words and Music by JOHN LENNON
and PAUL McCARTNEY

TIME AFTER TIME

TENOR SAX

Words and Music by CYNDI LAUPER
and ROB HYMAN

TIME IN A BOTTLE

TENOR SAX

Words and Music by
JIM CROCE

TRAVELIN' MAN

TENOR SAX

Words and Music by
JERRY FULLER

25 OR 6 TO 4

TENOR SAX

Words and Music by
ROBERT LAMM

Moderately fast

UP, UP AND AWAY

TENOR SAX

Words and Music by
JIMMY WEBB

WE'RE NOT GONNA TAKE IT

TENOR SAX

Words and Music by
DANIEL DEE SNIDER

WHAT'S LOVE GOT TO DO WITH IT

TENOR SAX

Words and Music by GRAHAM LYLE
and TERRY BRITTEN

A WHITER SHADE OF PALE

TENOR SAX

Words and Music by KEITH REID,
GARY BROOKER and MATTHEW FISHER

WICHITA LINEMAN

TENOR SAX

Words and Music by
JIMMY WEBB

Moderately slow

WITH OR WITHOUT YOU

TENOR SAX

Words and Music by
U2

YESTERDAY

TENOR SAX

Words and Music by JOHN LENNON
and PAUL McCARTNEY

Moderately, with expression

YOU ARE SO BEAUTIFUL

TENOR SAX

Words and Music by BILLY PRESTON
and BRUCE FISHER

YOU CAN'T HURRY LOVE

TENOR SAX

Words and Music by EDWARD HOLLAND JR.,
LAMONT DOZIER and BRIAN HOLLAND

YOU REALLY GOT ME

TENOR SAX

Words and Music by
RAY DAVIES

YOU'RE SO VAIN

TENOR SAX

Words and Music by
CARLY SIMON

101 SONGS

BIG COLLECTIONS OF FAVORITE SONGS ARRANGED FOR SOLO INSTRUMENTALISTS.

101 BROADWAY SONGS

00154199	Flute	$15.99
00154200	Clarinet	$15.99
00154201	Alto Sax	$15.99
00154202	Tenor Sax	$16.99
00154203	Trumpet	$15.99
00154204	Horn	$15.99
00154205	Trombone	$15.99
00154206	Violin	$15.99
00154207	Viola	$15.99
00154208	Cello	$15.99

101 DISNEY SONGS

00244104	Flute	$17.99
00244106	Clarinet	$17.99
00244107	Alto Sax	$17.99
00244108	Tenor Sax	$17.99
00244109	Trumpet	$17.99
00244112	Horn	$17.99
00244120	Trombone	$17.99
00244121	Violin	$17.99
00244125	Viola	$17.99
00244126	Cello	$17.99

101 MOVIE HITS

00158087	Flute	$15.99
00158088	Clarinet	$15.99
00158089	Alto Sax	$15.99
00158090	Tenor Sax	$15.99
00158091	Trumpet	$15.99
00158092	Horn	$15.99
00158093	Trombone	$15.99
00158094	Violin	$15.99
00158095	Viola	$15.99
00158096	Cello	$15.99

101 CHRISTMAS SONGS

00278637	Flute	$15.99
00278638	Clarinet	$15.99
00278639	Alto Sax	$15.99
00278640	Tenor Sax	$15.99
00278641	Trumpet	$15.99
00278642	Horn	$14.99
00278643	Trombone	$15.99
00278644	Violin	$15.99
00278645	Viola	$15.99
00278646	Cello	$15.99

101 HIT SONGS

00194561	Flute	$17.99
00197182	Clarinet	$17.99
00197183	Alto Sax	$17.99
00197184	Tenor Sax	$17.99
00197185	Trumpet	$17.99
00197186	Horn	$17.99
00197187	Trombone	$17.99
00197188	Violin	$17.99
00197189	Viola	$17.99
00197190	Cello	$17.99

101 POPULAR SONGS

00224722	Flute	$17.99
00224723	Clarinet	$17.99
00224724	Alto Sax	$17.99
00224725	Tenor Sax	$17.99
00224726	Trumpet	$17.99
00224727	Horn	$17.99
00224728	Trombone	$17.99
00224729	Violin	$17.99
00224730	Viola	$17.99
00224731	Cello	$17.99

101 CLASSICAL THEMES

00155315	Flute	$15.99
00155317	Clarinet	$15.99
00155318	Alto Sax	$15.99
00155319	Tenor Sax	$15.99
00155320	Trumpet	$15.99
00155321	Horn	$15.99
00155322	Trombone	$15.99
00155323	Violin	$15.99
00155324	Viola	$15.99
00155325	Cello	$15.99

101 JAZZ SONGS

00146363	Flute	$15.99
00146364	Clarinet	$15.99
00146366	Alto Sax	$15.99
00146367	Tenor Sax	$15.99
00146368	Trumpet	$15.99
00146369	Horn	$14.99
00146370	Trombone	$15.99
00146371	Violin	$15.99
00146372	Viola	$15.99
00146373	Cello	$15.99

101 MOST BEAUTIFUL SONGS

00291023	Flute	$16.99
00291041	Clarinet	$16.99
00291042	Alto Sax	$17.99
00291043	Tenor Sax	$17.99
00291044	Trumpet	$16.99
00291045	Horn	$16.99
00291046	Trombone	$16.99
00291047	Violin	$16.99
00291048	Viola	$16.99
00291049	Cello	$17.99

See complete song lists and sample pages at www.halleonard.com

HAL•LEONARD®
www.halleonard.com

Prices, contents and availability subject to change without notice.

HAL•LEONARD INSTRUMENTAL PLAY-ALONG

Your favorite songs are arranged just for solo instrumentalists with this outstanding series. Each book includes great full-accompaniment play-along audio so you can sound just like a pro!

Check out **halleonard.com** for songlists and more titles!

12 Pop Hits
12 songs
00261790	Flute	00261795	Horn
00261791	Clarinet	00261796	Trombone
00261792	Alto Sax	00261797	Violin
00261793	Tenor Sax	00261798	Viola
00261794	Trumpet	00261799	Cello

The Very Best of Bach
15 selections
00225371	Flute	00225376	Horn
00225372	Clarinet	00225377	Trombone
00225373	Alto Sax	00225378	Violin
00225374	Tenor Sax	00225379	Viola
00225375	Trumpet	00225380	Cello

The Beatles
15 songs
00225330	Flute	00225335	Horn
00225331	Clarinet	00225336	Trombone
00225332	Alto Sax	00225337	Violin
00225333	Tenor Sax	00225338	Viola
00225334	Trumpet	00225339	Cello

Chart Hits
12 songs
00146207	Flute	00146212	Horn
00146208	Clarinet	00146213	Trombone
00146209	Alto Sax	00146214	Violin
00146210	Tenor Sax	00146211	Trumpet
00146216	Cello		

Christmas Songs
12 songs
00146855	Flute	00146863	Horn
00146858	Clarinet	00146864	Trombone
00146859	Alto Sax	00146866	Violin
00146860	Tenor Sax	00146867	Viola
00146862	Trumpet	00146868	Cello

Contemporary Broadway
15 songs
00298704	Flute	00298709	Horn
00298705	Clarinet	00298710	Trombone
00298706	Alto Sax	00298711	Violin
00298707	Tenor Sax	00298712	Viola
00298708	Trumpet	00298713	Cello

Disney Movie Hits
12 songs
00841420	Flute	00841424	Horn
00841687	Oboe	00841425	Trombone
00841421	Clarinet	00841426	Violin
00841422	Alto Sax	00841427	Viola
00841686	Tenor Sax	00841428	Cello
00841423	Trumpet		

*Prices, contents, and availability
subject to change without notice.*

Disney characters and artwork ™ & © 2021 Disney

Disney Solos
12 songs
00841404	Flute	00841506	Oboe
00841406	Alto Sax	00841409	Trumpet
00841407	Horn	00841410	Violin
00841411	Viola	00841412	Cello
00841405	Clarinet/Tenor Sax		
00841408	Trombone/Baritone		
00841553	Mallet Percussion		

Dixieland Favorites
15 songs
00268756	Flute	0068759	Trumpet
00268757	Clarinet	00268760	Trombone
00268758	Alto Sax		

Billie Eilish
9 songs
00345648	Flute	00345653	Horn
00345649	Clarinet	00345654	Trombone
00345650	Alto Sax	00345655	Violin
00345651	Tenor Sax	00345656	Viola
00345652	Trumpet	00345657	Cello

Favorite Movie Themes
13 songs
00841166	Flute	00841168	Trumpet
00841167	Clarinet	00841170	Trombone
00841169	Alto Sax	00841296	Violin

Gospel Hymns
15 songs
00194648	Flute	00194654	Trombone
00194649	Clarinet	00194655	Violin
00194650	Alto Sax	00194656	Viola
00194651	Tenor Sax	00194657	Cello
00194652	Trumpet		

Great Classical Themes
15 songs
00292727	Flute	00292733	Horn
00292728	Clarinet	00292735	Trombone
00292729	Alto Sax	00292736	Violin
00292730	Tenor Sax	00292737	Viola
00292732	Trumpet	00292738	Cello

The Greatest Showman
8 songs
00277389	Flute	00277394	Horn
00277390	Clarinet	00277395	Trombone
00277391	Alto Sax	00277396	Violin
00277392	Tenor Sax	00277397	Viola
00277393	Trumpet	00277398	Cello

Irish Favorites
31 songs
00842489	Flute	00842495	Trombone
00842490	Clarinet	00842496	Violin
00842491	Alto Sax	00842497	Viola
00842493	Trumpet	00842498	Cello
00842494	Horn		

Michael Jackson
11 songs
00119495	Flute	00119499	Trumpet
00119496	Clarinet	00119501	Trombone
00119497	Alto Sax	00119503	Violin
00119498	Tenor Sax	00119502	Accomp.

Jazz & Blues
14 songs
00841438	Flute	00841441	Trumpet
00841439	Clarinet	00841443	Trombone
00841440	Alto Sax	00841444	Violin
00841442	Tenor Sax		

Jazz Classics
12 songs
00151812	Flute	00151816	Trumpet
00151813	Clarinet	00151818	Trombone
00151814	Alto Sax	00151819	Violin
00151815	Tenor Sax	00151821	Cello

Les Misérables
13 songs
00842292	Flute	00842297	Horn
00842293	Clarinet	00842298	Trombone
00842294	Alto Sax	00842299	Violin
00842295	Tenor Sax	00842300	Viola
00842296	Trumpet	00842301	Cello

Metallica
12 songs
02501327	Flute	02502454	Horn
02501339	Clarinet	02501329	Trombone
02501332	Alto Sax	02501334	Violin
02501333	Tenor Sax	02501335	Viola
02501330	Trumpet	02501338	Cello

Motown Classics
15 songs
00842572	Flute	00842576	Trumpet
00842573	Clarinet	00842578	Trombone
00842574	Alto Sax	00842579	Violin
00842575	Tenor Sax		

Pirates of the Caribbean
16 songs
00842183	Flute	00842188	Horn
00842184	Clarinet	00842189	Trombone
00842185	Alto Sax	00842190	Violin
00842186	Tenor Sax	00842191	Viola
00842187	Trumpet	00842192	Cello

Queen
17 songs
00285402	Flute	00285407	Horn
00285403	Clarinet	00285408	Trombone
00285404	Alto Sax	00285409	Violin
00285405	Tenor Sax	00285410	Viola
00285406	Trumpet	00285411	Cello

Simple Songs
14 songs
00249081	Flute	00249087	Horn
00249093	Oboe	00249089	Trombone
00249082	Clarinet	00249090	Violin
00249083	Alto Sax	00249091	Viola
00249084	Tenor Sax	00249092	Cello
00249086	Trumpet	00249094	Mallets

Superhero Themes
14 songs
00363195	Flute	00363200	Horn
00363196	Clarinet	00363201	Trombone
00363197	Alto Sax	00363202	Violin
00363198	Tenor Sax	00363203	Viola
00363199	Trumpet	00363204	Cello

Star Wars
16 songs
00350900	Flute	00350907	Horn
00350913	Oboe	00350908	Trombone
00350903	Clarinet	00350909	Violin
00350904	Alto Sax	00350910	Viola
00350905	Tenor Sax	00350911	Cello
00350906	Trumpet	00350914	Mallet

Taylor Swift
15 songs
00842532	Flute	00842537	Horn
00842533	Clarinet	00842538	Trombone
00842534	Alto Sax	00842539	Violin
00842535	Tenor Sax	00842540	Viola
00842536	Trumpet	00842541	Cello

Video Game Music
13 songs
00283877	Flute	00283883	Horn
00283878	Clarinet	00283884	Trombone
00283879	Alto Sax	00283885	Violin
00283880	Tenor Sax	00283886	Viola
00283882	Trumpet	00283887	Cello

Wicked
13 songs
00842236	Flute	00842241	Horn
00842237	Clarinet	00842242	Trombone
00842238	Alto Sax	00842243	Violin
00842239	Tenor Sax	00842244	Viola
00842240	Trumpet	00842245	Cello

HAL•LEONARD®

101 TIPS FROM HAL LEONARD

STUFF ALL THE PROS KNOW AND USE

Ready to take your skills to the next level? These books present valuable how-to insight that musicians of all styles and levels can benefit from. The text, photos, music, diagrams and accompanying audio provide a terrific, easy-to-use resource for a variety of topics.

101 HAMMOND B-3 TIPS
by Brian Charette
Topics include: funky scales and modes; unconventional harmonies; creative chord voicings; cool drawbar settings; ear-grabbing special effects; professional gigging advice; practicing effectively; making good use of the pedals; and much more!
00128918 Book/Online Audio $14.99

101 HARMONICA TIPS
by Steve Cohen
Topics include: techniques, position playing, soloing, accompaniment, the blues, equipment, performance, maintenance, and much more!
00821040 Book/Online Audio $17.99

101 CELLO TIPS—2ND EDITION
by Angela Schmidt
Topics include: bowing techniques, non-classical playing, electric cellos, accessories, gig tips, practicing, recording and much more!
00149094 Book/Online Audio $14.99

101 FLUTE TIPS
by Elaine Schmidt
Topics include: selecting the right flute for you, finding the right teacher, warm-up exercises, practicing effectively, taking good care of your flute, gigging advice, staying and playing healthy, and much more.
00119883 Book/CD Pack....................................$14.99

101 SAXOPHONE TIPS
by Eric Morones
Topics include: techniques; maintenance; equipment; practicing; recording; performance; and much more!
00311082 Book/CD Pack....................................$19.99

101 TRUMPET TIPS
by Scott Barnard
Topics include: techniques, articulation, tone production, soloing, exercises, special effects, equipment, performance, maintenance and much more.
00312082 Book/CD Pack....................................$14.99

101 UPRIGHT BASS TIPS
by Andy McKee
Topics include: right- and left-hand technique, improvising and soloing, practicing, proper care of the instrument, ear training, performance, and much more.
00102009 Book/Online Audio $14.99

101 BASS TIPS
by Gary Willis
Topics include: techniques, improvising and soloing, equipment, practicing, ear training, performance, theory, and much more.
00695542 Book/Online Audio $19.99

101 DRUM TIPS—2ND EDITION
Topics include: grooves, practicing, warming up, tuning, gear, performance, and much more!
00151936 Book/Online Audio $14.99

101 FIVE-STRING BANJO TIPS
by Fred Sokolow
Topics include: techniques, ear training, performance, and much more!
00696647 Book/CD Pack....................................$14.99

101 GUITAR TIPS
by Adam St. James
Topics include: scales, music theory, truss rod adjustments, proper recording studio set-ups, and much more. The book also features snippets of advice from some of the most celebrated guitarists and producers in the music business.
00695737 Book/Online Audio $17.99

101 MANDOLIN TIPS
by Fred Sokolow
Topics include: playing tips, practicing tips, accessories, mandolin history and lore, practical music theory, and much more!
00119493 Book/Online Audio $14.99

101 RECORDING TIPS
by Adam St. James
This book contains recording tips, suggestions, and advice learned firsthand from legendary producers, engineers, and artists. These tricks of the trade will improve anyone's home or pro studio recordings.
00311035 Book/CD Pack....................................$14.95

101 UKULELE TIPS
by Fred Sokolow with Ronny Schiff
Topics include: techniques, improvising and soloing, equipment, practicing, ear training, performance, uke history and lore, and much more!
00696596 Book/Online Audio $15.99

101 VIOLIN TIPS
by Angela Schmidt
Topics include: bowing techniques, non-classical playing, electric violins, accessories, gig tips, practicing, recording, and much more!
00842672 Book/CD Pack....................................$14.99

Prices, contents and availability subject to change without notice.

HAL•LEONARD®
www.halleonard.com